All Kinds of Babies

Linda M. Washington

A Harcourt Achieve Imprint

www.Rigby.com
1-800-531-5015

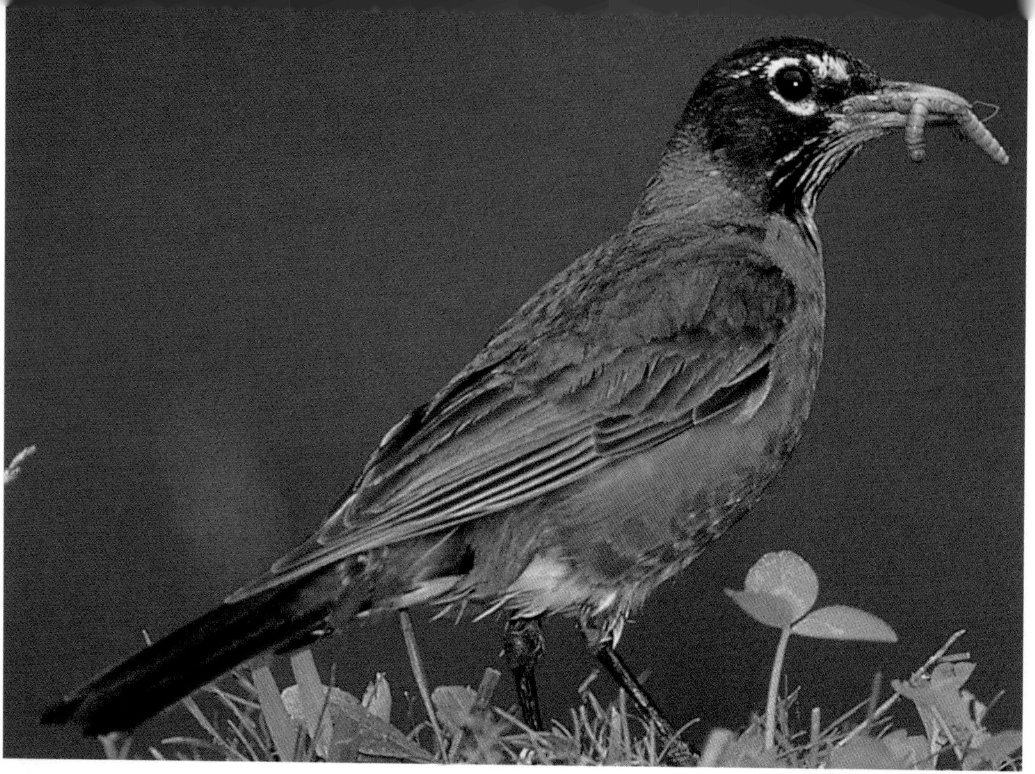

Here is a mother bird.

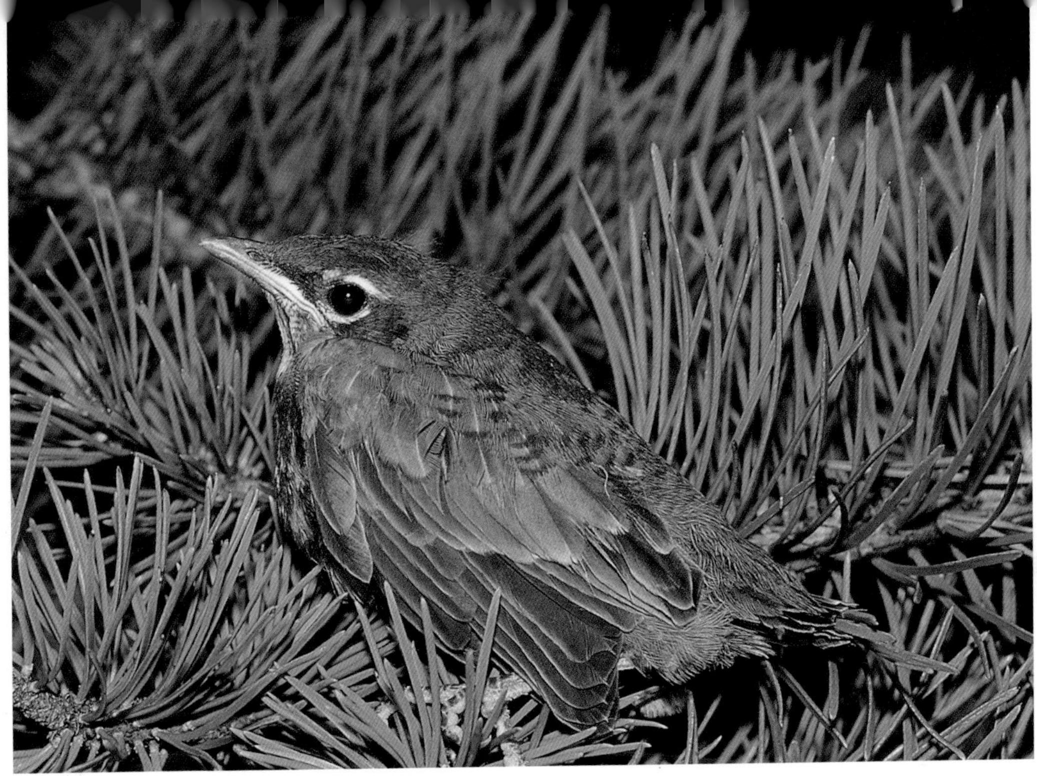

Here is her baby.

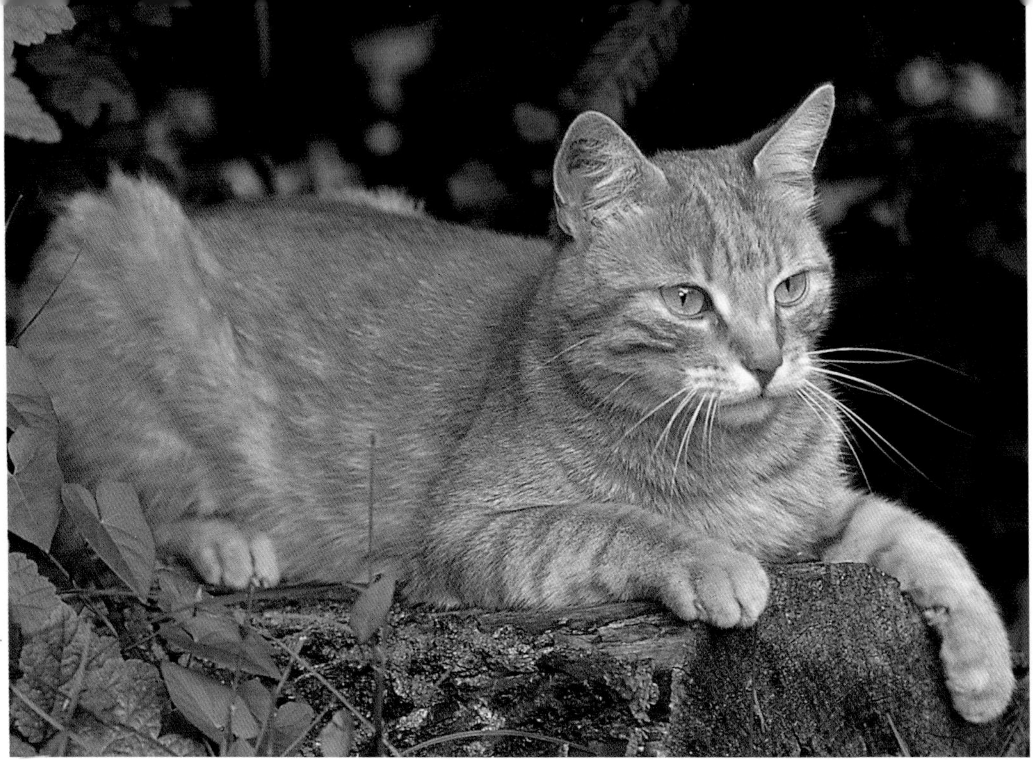

Here is a mother cat.

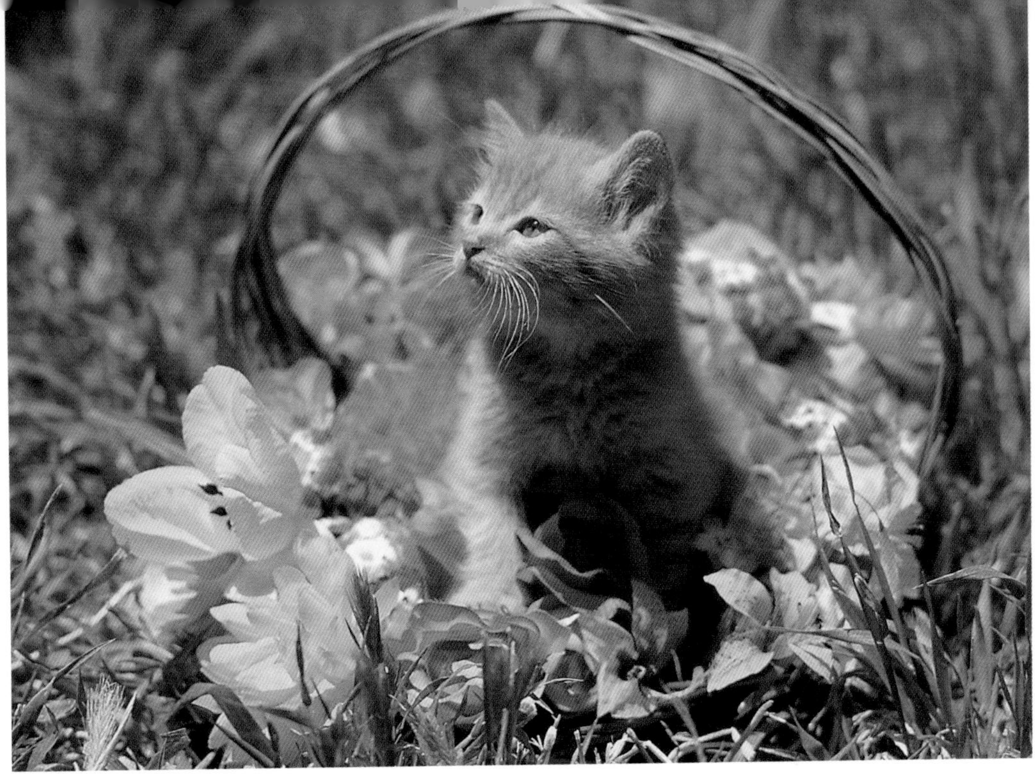

Here is her baby.

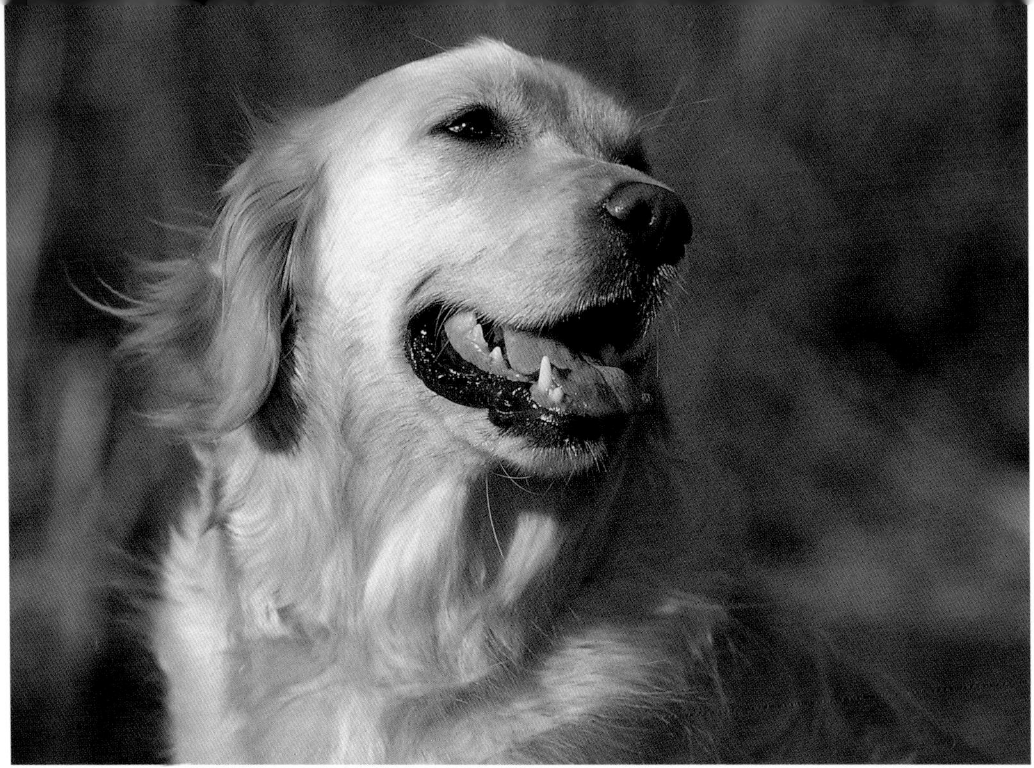

Here is a mother dog.

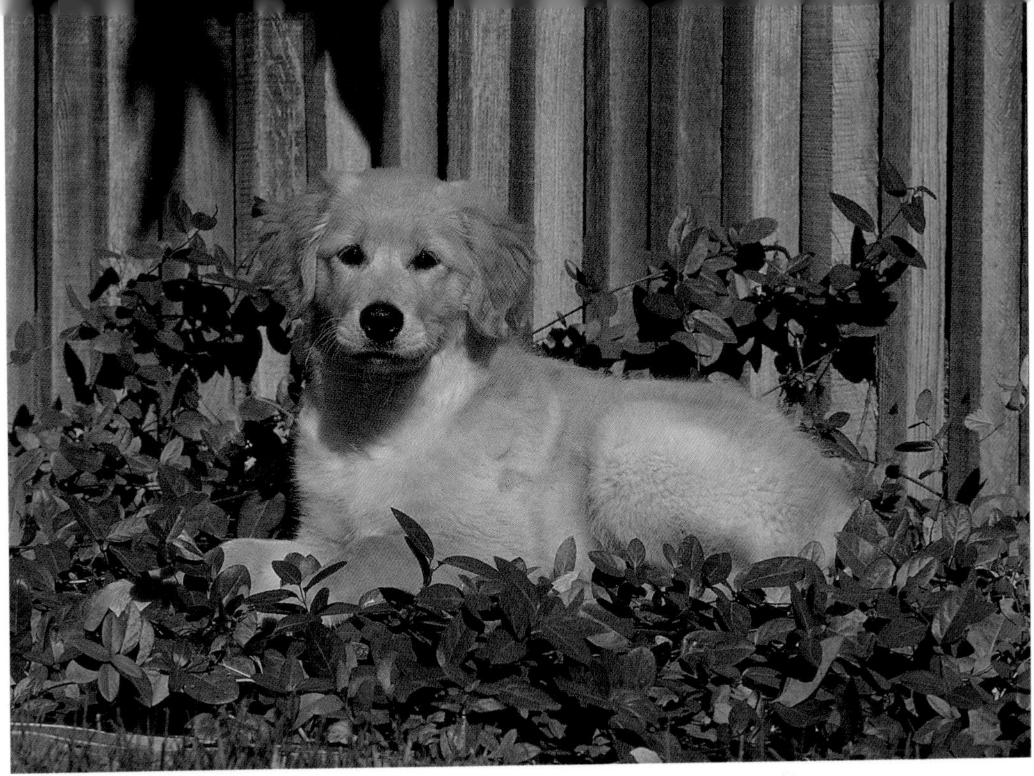

Here is her baby.

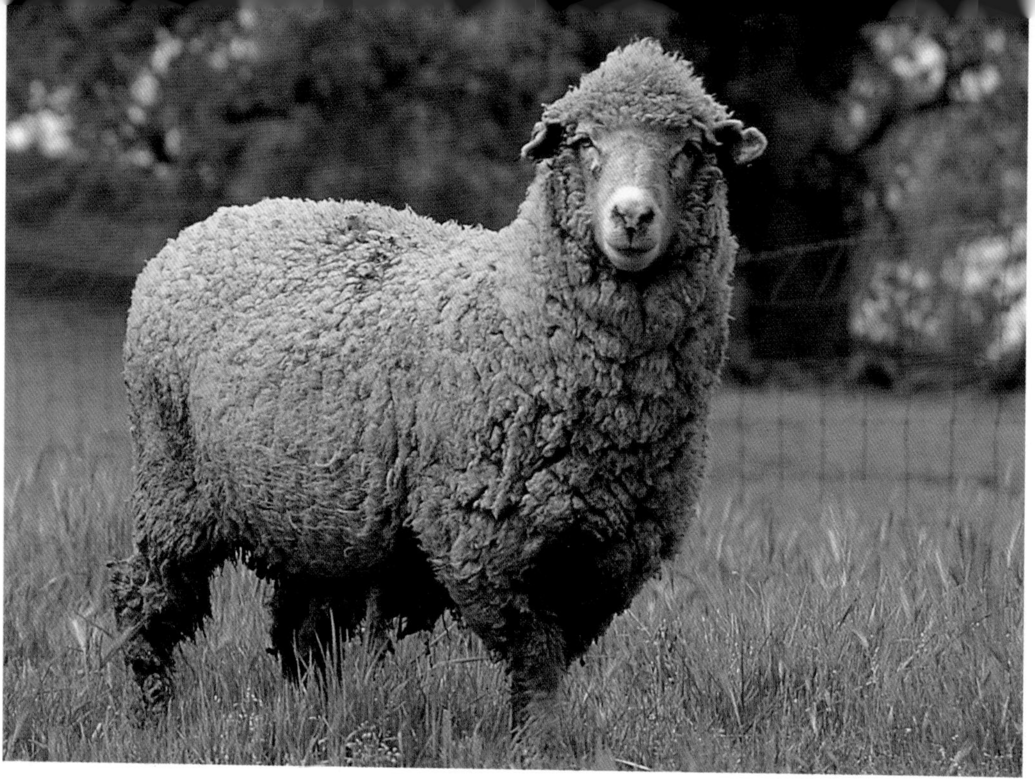

Here is a mother sheep.

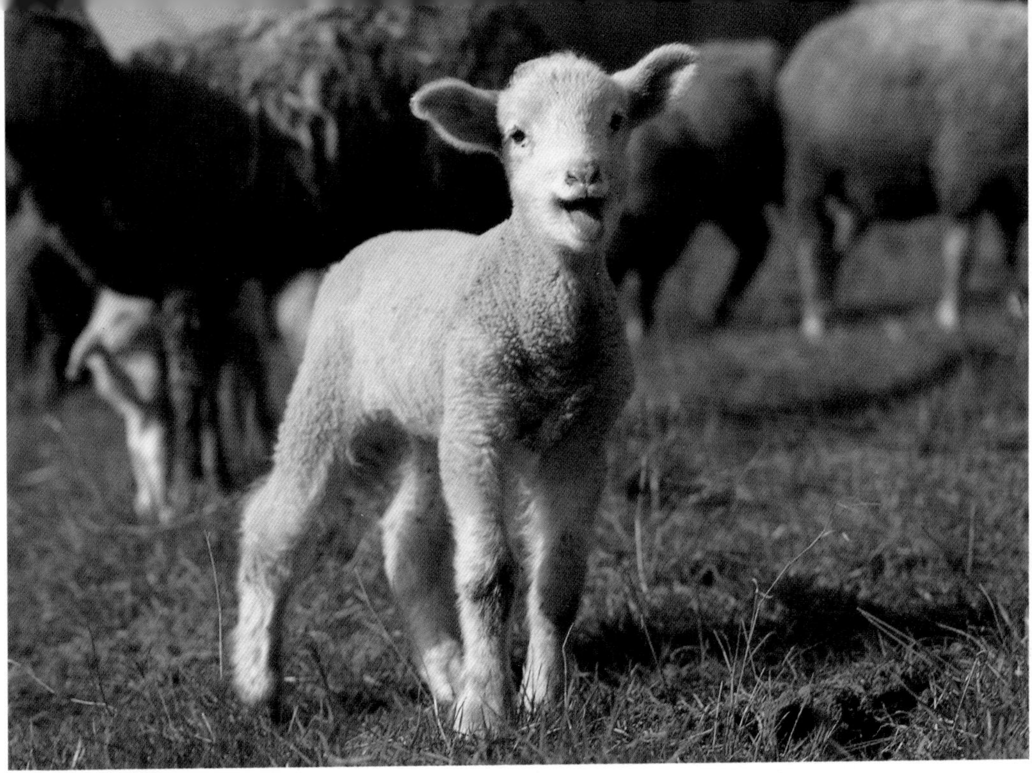

Here is her baby.

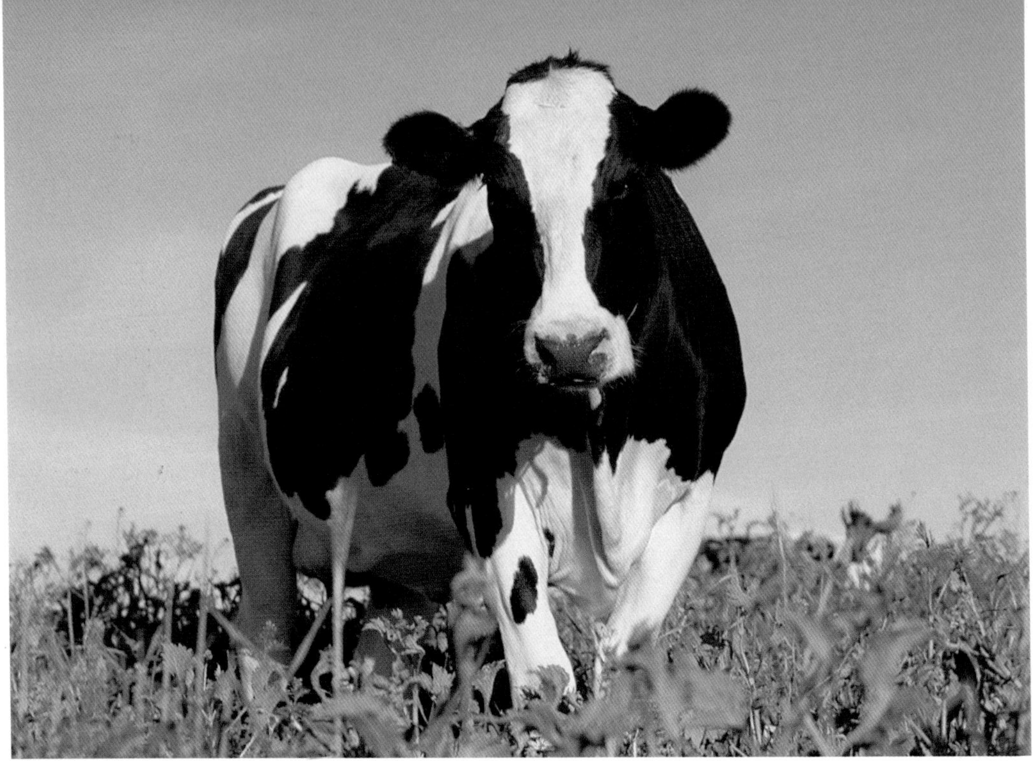

Here is a mother cow.

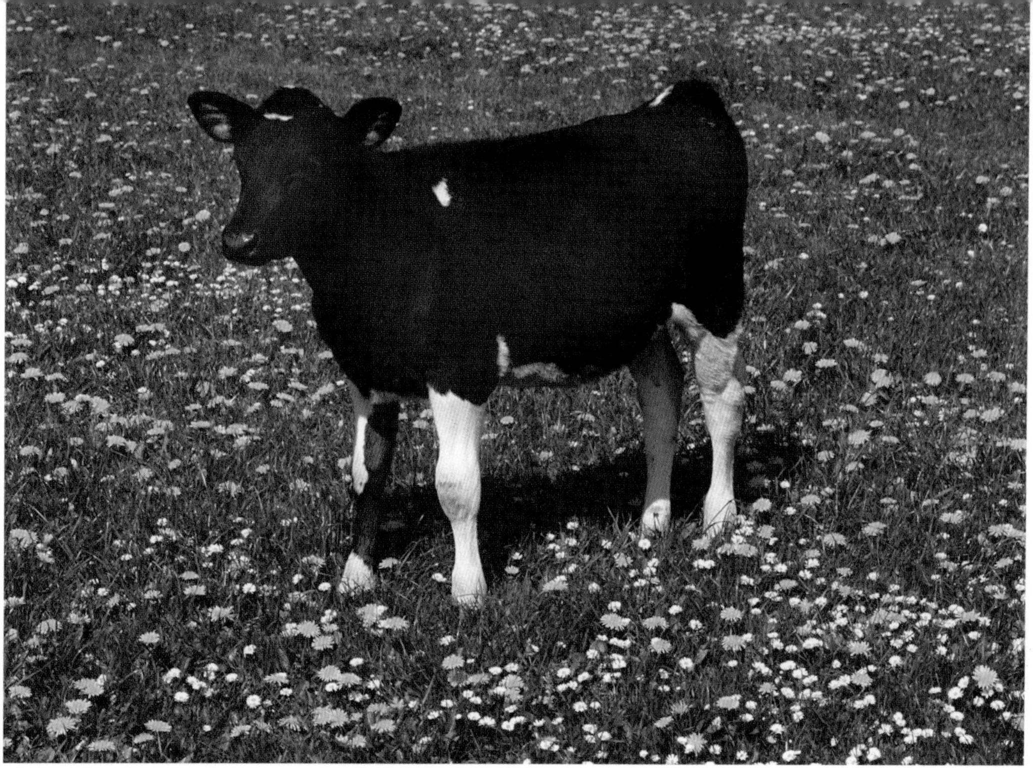

Here is her baby.

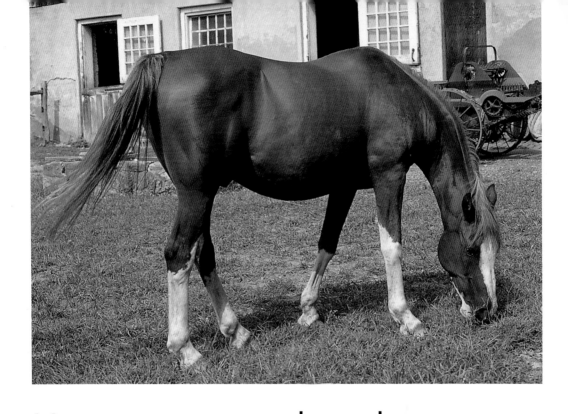

Here is a mother horse.

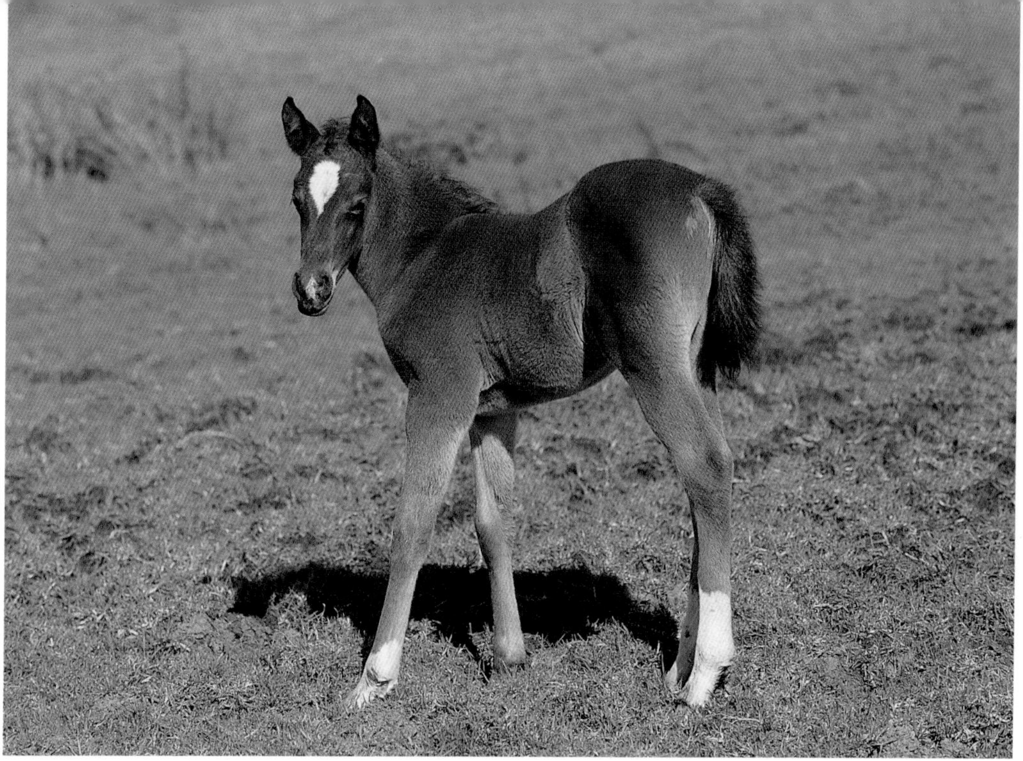

Here is her baby.

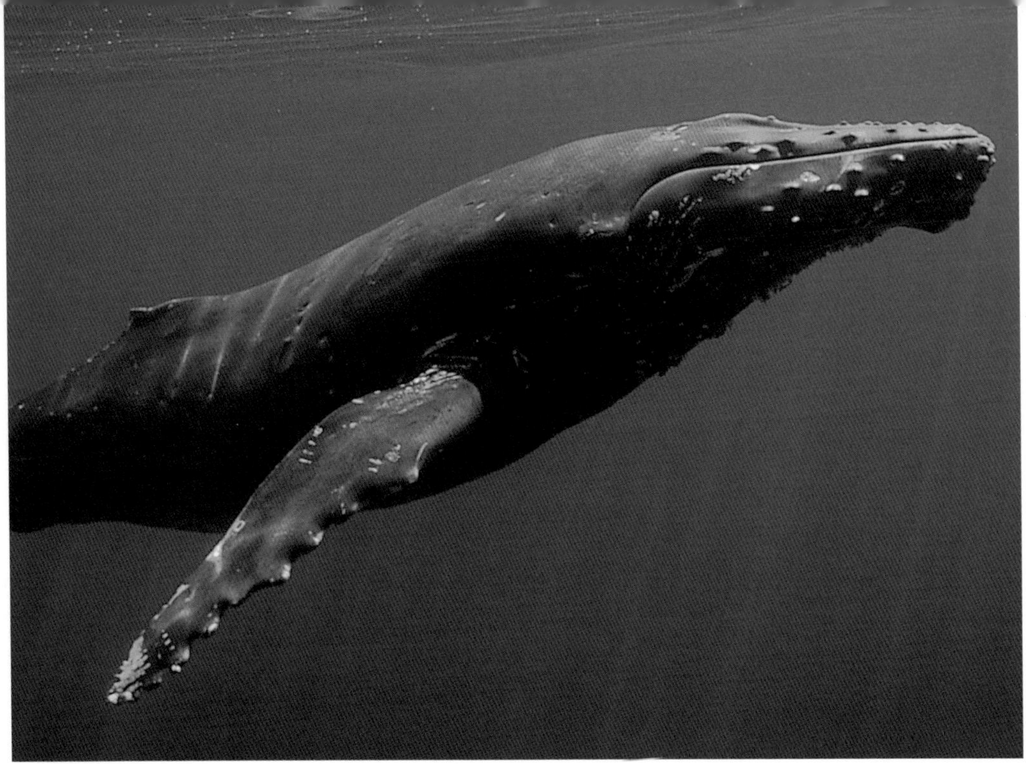

Here is a mother whale.

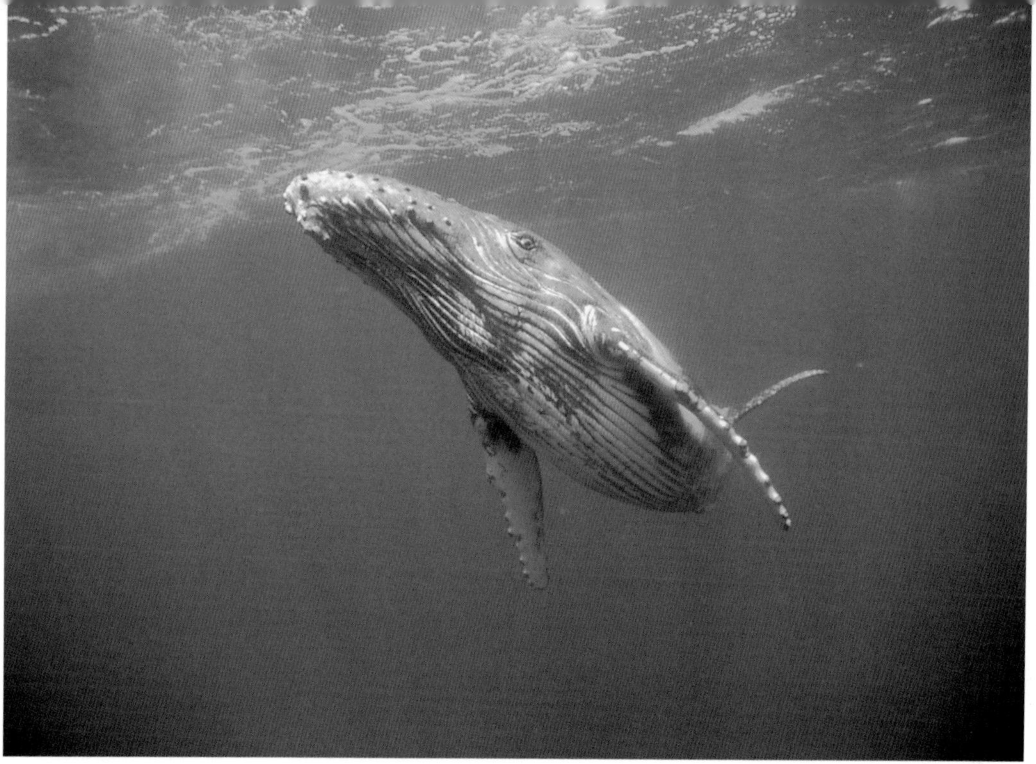

Here is her baby.

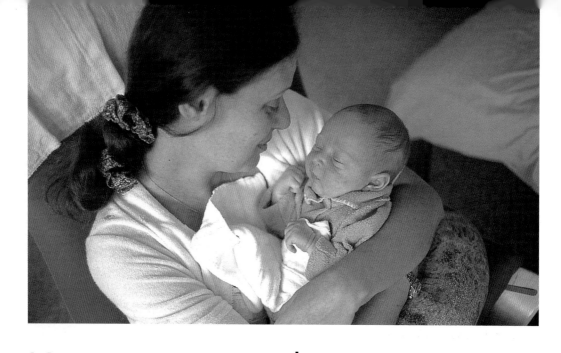

Here is a mother.

Here is her baby.